BLUU Notes

BLUU Notes

An Anthology of Love, Justice, and Liberation

Edited by Takiyah Nur Amin
and Mykal Slack

Black Lives of Unitarian Universalism (BLUU)
and Skinner House Books
Boston

skinnerhouse.org
blacklivesuu.org

Printed in the United States

Text and cover design by Tim Holtz
Photo of Takiyah Amin by C. Laughinghouse

print ISBN: 978-1-55896-880-6
eBook ISBN: 978-1-55896-881-3

6 5 4 3 2 1
26 25 24 23 22 21

Cataloging-in-Publication information on file with the Library of Congress

Contents

Introduction

At Black Lives of Unitarian Universalism (BLUU), both as an organization and as a growing spiritual family, we understand Unitarian Universalism as an orientation toward love and self-love, toward justice and liberation, and toward a call to relationship building that is grounded in accountability and care, all centered in Blackness and all with a belief in the power and possibility of Unitarian Universalism living up to the very best parts of itself. Our perspective centers our Seven Principles of Black Lives, which you will find at the end of this introduction; the Seven Principles of Unitarian Universalism, from which we drew inspiration for our principled recrafting; wisdom from many sources, including the six that have been a hallmark of Unitarian Universalism; and the wealth of experiences, sacred texts, and practices that we bring as Black people.

As you will notice in this anthology, we embrace multi-religiosity, spiritual fluidity, and complex faith identity. Many of our Black predecessors in the

Unitarian Universalist tradition held memberships in multiple communities of faith to cobble together space to hold their multifaceted theological perspectives and commitments to justice making. We build BLUU spaces because they keep us from needing to do the same, endeavoring to make room for all that we bring as Black people.

How to Use This Book

Our hope is that you will use this book to accompany you during your personal moments of worship, meditation, and reflection. The offerings in this volume are meant to sustain and encourage you as you journey toward deepening and growing your faith. We hope you will use this resource intentionally and share its depth and beauty as you find opportunity. Note that all the words you read here come from the lives, hearts, and multiple perspectives of Black UUs. The goal is not to present a seamless singular narrative but rather to support the spiritual and pastoral needs of our diverse and ever-growing community through a shared resource steeped in our growing articulation of a Black Unitarian Universalism.

About Black Lives of Unitarian Universalism

Our Beliefs

We articulate a Black Unitarian Universalism that is not dogmatic and does not prescribe a particular belief. One may embrace a range of spiritual truths or no faith at all; we acknowledge that one might believe many things over time. Our diverse beliefs and understandings of faith and connection must reflect the richness of our experiences as diasporic people. We believe in the possibility of that which has never been tested in the ways we're testing it. We believe in investing in people, ideas, organizing, theologies, *be*-ologies, *do* ologies, and Black futures where supremacy and colonization have no place and cannot thrive. And we believe in showing up in our communities in ways that uphold, amplify, and affirm Black life.

We believe that a faithful witness in Unitarian Universalism is not individualistic but relational, and that the evidence of our beliefs is shown in the depth and quality of our relationships. We learn from and wrestle with our faith and human connection not in isolation but in accountable relationship and deep covenant with each other and our local communities. We have a responsibility to be present for and with each other across the generations and other markers of difference—not just to receive but also to give. As such, we believe in directing our time, our money, and our talents toward efforts that foster this understanding.

We believe in sharing what gives our lives meaning. Therefore, we support proselytizing and evangelizing a Black Unitarian Universalist worldview that shares the good news of a faith that liberates and orients us to freedom.

We reject the notion that to be a Black Unitarian Universalist is to believe in anything you want and/or nothing in particular. Ours is not an "at least" faith whereby we assess our commitments based on the whims of the moment. Rather, we embrace this living tradition as one that requires ongoing reflection and deep wrestling with our values so that we might reconcile them with how we live in the world. We understand progress as something measured by proximity to our ideals, not distance from our worst moral failings. To live fully into this tradition, we do not believe in checking any part of ourselves at the door to participate in this faith—rather, we must bring our whole thinking, doing, breathing, reflecting selves to the practice of Unitarian Universalism. Ours is not an anti-intellectual project.

We also don't necessarily need to have shared beliefs as much as we need a shared commitment to act in a world where we are all not yet free. Our Black Unitarian Universalism therefore asks us questions about the beliefs we espouse: Do your beliefs point you to liberation for Black people and all people? Do your beliefs point you to liberation, compassion, love, and justice? Do your beliefs foster communal well-being? Do your beliefs call you to actions that prioritize humanity as only one part of a complex web of existence? Do your beliefs invite you to love folks in the fullness of their complex identity? We are committed to an ongoing interrogation of our beliefs in the light of reason, experience, and expertise.

Our Inspiration

There are wise ways of knowing, innovating, and living in the skin and bones of Black people. That we are still here is a testament to that fact. We draw inspiration, direction, and provocation from our ancestors—including Black Unitarians, Black Universalists, and Black Unitarian Universalists—who forged pathways at the intersection of faith and justice. We see in their lives not just a timeline of historical facts or incidents but also evidence and source material for evaluating the ways we live our traditions. We are inspired by all they did with far less access to resources and information. We are directed by their lives because in them we see causes worthy of our attention and action, and we are provoked by their legacy to consider what issues of our time require our action as people of faith.

Our Worship

The word "worship" has had a uniquely complicated history in the broader tradition of Unitarian Universalism. And at the same time, this is a word that you'll routinely hear among many Black UUs. What do we mean when we use this term? What is worship? What do we worship when we gather in community or in private times of reverence? Quite simply, we worship the holy. That thing that unites us and the energy/spirit that binds us. We worship that which arrives to call us into a deeper relationship with and care for one another, the spirit of life that arises in community that can't be explained totally in words or contained in any singular tradition. Some call it God, some don't call it anything at all, and the wide swath of understanding within and beyond these perspectives is too bountiful to attempt here in these pages.

We also recognize that there are many words that refer to honoring the holy within, among, and around us. "Worship" is only one of those words. Whatever words we use as Black UUs to express these ideas, we always endeavor to make a space elastic, dynamic, love-centered, and worthy enough of our full diasporic humanity. BLUU spaces will always foster a culture of mutuality, respect, and consent.

Our Transformation

This growing conceptualization of Black Unitarian Universalism offers a deep and abiding engagement with transformation. Mainstream faith sells the idea that it's perfectly fine to come and be here exactly as you are, never changing anything. What we are saying as Black

UUs is that this faith calls us to the kind of transformation that the work of faith demands. That is to say that being in community requires that we are open to making sacrifices, getting uncomfortable, existing differently, communicating differently, and loving more fully and deeply in a world that situates us as accomplices to systems of oppression. It matters that we, according to the mandate articulated by Mary Hooks of Southerners on New Ground, are being "transformed in the service of the work." And we believe in the capacity of ourselves and each other to grow, change, and shift toward ever-increasing frameworks of love and justice.

This faith does not belong to us, nor does it belong to anyone else. And yet we have a responsibility to Unitarian Universalism and to Black people to help bring it to life and give it some shape that we can live and lean into—not just for our own sakes, but also for the sakes of all those who have not arrived yet and to help us all change the world. Dr. Elías Ortega, president of Meadville Lombard Theological School, put it best when he said,

> One cannot own a faith because faith is not
> a possession that can circulate like a good to

be consumed, purchased, sold, or collected. But one can live into a faith, be transformed by it, be accountable to it in community.

Our Vision Statement reminds us that "BLUU harnesses love's power to combat oppression and foster healing as a spiritual and political imperative. We know the power of love to be life changing, inclusive, relational, uncomfortable, unconditional and without end."

May this power of love you find in these pages change your life and your Unitarian Universalism. May this power of love remind you (we are talking to every person who finds something meaningful in this anthology, and we are especially talking to every Black and Indigenous person and every person of color here) that every ounce of what makes you *you* is welcome and celebrated here. May this power of love grow relationships beyond your wildest dreams. May this power of love call us into a sacred discomfort that will make us better and brighter humans in a world where we are all not yet free. May you know this power of love in the depths of your heart, mind, body, and spirit. And may this power of love never leave you and take up residence in all the places you call home. Thank you for picking up this resource and for sharing it with the people who mean something to you in this life. We hope that there is something in it for all of us.

As an entry point and a way to settle into who and what you will find in the pages (read: hearts, minds, spirits, and lived experiences) that follow, here are BLUU's Seven Principles of Black Lives, the very first articulation of who we are and what we believe. They were launched over social media in September of 2015. We are forever indebted to the Movement for Black Lives and their framing and to the people who put these words and sentiments together: Leslie Mac, Lena Katherine Gardner, Kenny Wiley, Elandria Williams (1979–2020), and Rev. Carlton E. Smith.

Seven Principles of Black Lives

Principle 1: All Black Lives Matter

Queer Black lives, trans Black lives, formerly incarcerated Black lives, differently abled Black lives, Black women's lives, immigrant Black lives, Black elderly and children's lives. ALL BLACK LIVES MATTER and are creators of this space. We throw no one under the bus. We rise together.

The Movement for Black Lives calls on the Unitarian Universalist faith—a faith willing to make the bold proclamation that each person inherently matters—to live up to that claim by working toward a future in which Black lives are truly valued in our society. We call on UUs to actively resist notions that Black lives only matter if conformed to white, middle-class norms and to challenge assumptions of worth centered around clothing, diction, education, or other status. Our value is not conditional.

Principle 2: **Love and Self-Love Are Practiced in Every Element of All We Do**

Love and self-love must be drivers of all our work and indicators of our success. Without these principles and without healing, we will harm each other and undermine our movement.

The Movement for Black Lives seeks to build a society where Black people thrive instead of survive. We seek justice for those we have lost to police violence; we seek equity in housing, education, and healthcare; we seek compassion from our fellow UUs for the struggle we are called to be a part of.

Principle 3: **Spiritual Growth Is Directly Tied to Our Ability to Embrace Our Whole Selves**

A principled struggle must exist in a positive environment. We must be honest with one another by embracing direct, loving communication and acknowledgment of all that we are and all that we hope to be.

The spiritual growth of UUs of color is directly tied to our ability to uphold the truth that Black Lives

Matter—that our lives matter both in the wider world and, just as important, in our UU congregations. We call on our UU congregations and the UUA to support our work toward wholeness as Black people. We must be honest with one another by embracing direct, loving communication.

Principle 4: Experimentation and Innovation Must Be Built into Our Work

We embrace the best tools, practices, and tactics and leave behind those that no longer serve us. Evaluation and assessment must be built into our work. Critical reflection must be part of all our work. We learn from our mistakes and our victories.

The Movement for Black Lives works daily to expose the truth about Black life in this country and in the world. To uncover the layer of white supremacy culture that exists in this society. To bring to light the anti-Blackness that is present in our everyday lives. We call on all UUs to root out the anti-Blackness that exists within our congregations and our faith.

Principle 5: The Most Directly Affected People Are Experts at Their Own Lives

Those most directly affected by racial injustice and oppression should be in leadership, at the center of our movement, and telling their stories directly.

We uphold the Movement for Black Lives at a time in which voting rights are being threatened at every turn. Black people are being denied the most basic of rights: the right to vote and the right to have adequate representation in our country. We work toward a society in which Black life is valued, in which Black life is not discarded, in which Black Lives Matter, and in which the work of Black people is seen as equal to that of their white counterparts. Black voices in our congregations, in our faith, and in the world must be valued.

Principle 6: Thriving Instead of Surviving

Our vision is based on the world we want and not the world we are currently in. We seek to transform, not simply to react. We want our people to thrive, not just exist—and to think beyond the possible.

Any work toward peace, liberty, and justice must address racial injustice. Black UUs are calling our faith to join us as we work toward justice for *all* Black people and, by extension, for all people.

Principle 7: **360-Degree Vision**

We honor the past struggles and present-day wisdom from our elders. The work we do today builds the foundations of the movements of tomorrow. We consider our mark on future generations.

Acknowledging the ways in which a Supremacist society diminishes us *all* is a critical part of the work of the Movement for Black Lives. When the most marginalized of our society are free, then we will *all* truly be free. We call on our faith to affirm the truth that only when Black Lives Matter will all lives *truly* matter. As Dr. King said, "Injustice anywhere is a threat to justice everywhere. We are caught in an inescapable network of mutuality, tied in a single garment of destiny. Whatever affects one directly, affects all indirectly."

OUR ENERGIES

Morning Song

PATRICE CURTIS

You.
Yes,
You right there, You reading this,

You are the spirit of the holy, face of the sacred:
your frail, strong, human body, the universe
manifest.
I give my thanks for You.

I turn my face and hands toward You to behold
and hold You
Precious.

My kindness lays upon You, and surrounds You;
And when I fail, frail myself,
I turn yet again and again,
to be gracious to You.

I am inseparable from You for all time,
from this life to the next and all that follow.

It has been so, it is so, and will be forevermore.

Prayer of Power and Wonder

MYKAL SLACK

Written for the 2019 Harper-Jordan Memorial Symposium

Spirit of Wonder and Power, Great Love that has wrapped us up in the magic of our presence here together, we offer our deep gratitude. . . .

For the Earth and the life in abundance she makes way for. For this moment and for these people. For the time we've already had here together to laugh, cry, break bread, cut up, learn, and grow together. For the things we always manage to do when we get together—open hearts, believe in the impossible, feel with our whole everything a joy too often unattainable when we're apart from one another. For all of the people in our lives whose prophetic words and deeds have paved the way for our dreams, our insights, and this very gathering to take place.

May this be a time to settle firmly into a simultaneous commitment to Black life and to Unitarian Universalism. May this gathering serve as an opportunity to bear witness to works of connection, relationship, and collaboration being done in a new way. May this be a powerful testament to our gifts, the richness of our lives, and our collective voice. May all that we are and all that we bring, every bit of joy and triumph and every ounce of uncertainty and heartache, carry us through, offer us every lesson we may need to be healing forces without our own selves, within our communities—here and beyond, and out in the world.

What a great blessing it is to be here together.

Ashe. Amen. Blessed be.

Invocation
EVERETT HOAGLAND

Architect of icebergs, rainbows.
Jeweler of crystals, sand grains, snowflakes, atoms.

Mason whose tools are glaciers, rain, rivers, ocean.

Chemist who made blood
of seawater, bone of minerals in stone, milk

of love. Whatever

you are, I know this:
Spinner, you are everywhere, in all the ever-
changing above, whirling around us.

Yes, in the loose strands,
in the rough weave of the common

cloth threaded with our DNA on the hubbed, spoked
spinning wheel that is this world, solar system, galaxy,

universe.

Help us to see ourselves in all creation,
and all creation in ourselves, Ourselves in One Another.

Remind those of us who like connections
made with similes, metaphors, symbols
that all of us are, everything is,
already connected.

Remind us that as the oceans go, so go we.
As the air goes, so go we.
As other life forms on Earth go, so go we.

As our planet goes, so go we. Mysterious Muse
who inspired "In the beginning was the word . . . ,"

edit our thoughts so our ethics are our politics,
and our actions the afterlives of our words.

Gather the Bones

SOFÍA BETANCOURT

for the ancestors whose funeral prayers I sang under
     the full moon
that night in Cuba by the water

What would it mean to sanctify you,
to dredge your fractured body
from the embrace of too-hard seas?
To gather the bones, child.
The bones.

Gather the bones, child,
for in them lies history,
voices long tortured,
nameless and forgotten,
their ancestral strength beyond measure.

Search for powdered traces, child,
left swirling in deep waters,
identities patterned like the
spore print of a mushroom,
like the fungal flower traces of the dead.

Speak the truth, child.
Our people came to rest
on the bottoms of oceans,
an amassed revolution of
skeletal fragments.

Where would your bones lie,
dragged bleeding and betrayed
chained to the bottoms of ships,
plotting freedom through the
blessed, dark, watery deep?

Could you find them today?

Or would you too whisper
words on the winds
calling to yourself in renewed flesh,
on strange lands, with peculiar words
calling to collect the tiniest bones?

To gather fragments littering beaches
of too-expensive resorts,
where those same sailors sun themselves,
towels spread on crumbled bodies,
to darken their own skins.

Do you recognize yourself
walking the sands at sunset?
Does your soul cry out on the winds to
gather the bones, child?
Gather the bones.

Toward a Place of Wholeness

Viola Abbitt

We are Unitarian Universalists.

When we lift up our Seven Principles, some of us think of them as a form of theology—but they are more important to our collective than that:
they do not tell us what we should believe; they tell us how we should be.

They tell us how we should act in the larger world and with each other.

We are brought here today by the fact that Unitarian Universalism has fallen short of the image that was presented to the world and to many of those who embraced this religion.

But we are also brought here today by the truth that Unitarian Universalism has shifted course to move toward a place of wholeness: a place that has perhaps never existed for us as a denomination.

It has been a long and sometimes unforgiving road to today. But we are here today because we are mindful of that past and because we have hope for the future. We want the practice of this faith to be a fulfilling manifestation of its promise.

Open your hearts. Seek new ways of understanding. Come, let us worship together.

Black Girl Blues

Melissa C. Jeter

I don't want to mourn Black girl blues,
though there are times I really want to be seen
I just really want to do my own thing.

Maybe I'll jump at the sun and smile knowing that
what's in my head and on my heart
is a beautiful work of art.

Sometimes, I get angry and internalize it;
I get real stubborn about what I know I am, about
what I know I have the skills to do.
I smirk when the people say *who knew*?

I could be invisible, and I thought for a long time
        that I was.
As I was looking out and they were looking upon,
what . . . what did they see?

Surely it was not Me, just projections of their
        imaginings and
proscriptive roles of enmeshment and
        co-dependency

Nah, they never really see me.
Because the eyes they do deceive
and their heart is never near to me

And their mind is so full of scientific designs and
    enlightenment;
they know so they are closed to me

So in many ways I am free
Free when I breathe deeply on my zafu
and face Tina, Black Jesus, the brown naked
    goddesses, the triune of scarf-covered,
brown-shaded women with hands upturned in
    prayer, as well as the storyteller figurine
on all fours covered in tiny children from Ecuador;
I am free when I read Susan Taylor, former editor of
    Essence,
Words that say *let go*

And I breathe out and see that love is truly free.
Just let go.
I straighten my back; my second chakra opens;
I listen and hear *Grow up*
I look at Tina and I hear her say, I don't really want to
    fight anymore
There are all kinds of people in this world,

Some will die for you, some will lie to you . . .
And then I am aurally directed to Ruthie singing Maya
Saying, pretty women wonder where my secret lies

I'm not cute or built to suit a fashion model size
But when I start to tell them they think I'm telling lies

One more deep breath
and I have centered myself for the
practice that is ineffable connection,
an assertion to That which flows through me
and every living thing.
I know it's true because that's when the cat cries out

I really won't mourn, though I sing the blues
Maya said that my ticket was bought
My ancestors paid the dues

Beloved Space

JAN CARPENTER TUCKER

Safe space . . .
An illusion
A magical myth
A place to suffer silently
Your free expression, my oppression
Your privilege, my pain
Step lightly, remind gently
Disarm, yet do no harm
Hold safe space so all are heard, and none are hurt
Hold the tongue so none are heard, and all are hurt

Brave space . . .
A hope
A prayer
A wish
A place where
Words are spoken
Tears shed
Hearts rendered
Dreams realized

Shared space . . .
Now feels unsafe
Growth demands new depths of comprehension
Wide berth for acceptance
Tougher skin
Steel-toed boots
To shield our weary, marching, stepped-on feet

Sanctuary for unconditional love
Replete with conditions
Your building up might tear me down
Your tearing down might kill me
What foundation exists
To fill the voids
Crowd out the noise
To make this place, this space
Beloved?

If love holds power
How much will it take to
Be love, breathe love, be loved, Beloveds
In this Beloved Space?

The Change

MATHEW P. TAYLOR

I can feel the change coming
Like growing pains
I feel the change in my bones
Pulling me
Stretching me
Forming me
Into the true *I am*
Can you feel it?

The change in our bodies
As we adapt
Grow
Change
The weight shifting and molding to fit
This evolving body that we are in
Guided by faith that this too will pass
We can survive this because our ancestors survived
Can you feel them in your DNA?

You, a mixture of their particles that was molded to
        fit your spirit
Change and shift
Mold and grow
Yet in some ways
we stay the same

God Knows My Name

QIYAMAH RAHMAN

God knows my name

She hears me in the midnight hour and all through the day

I speak my name and give thanks and spit my name into the vast oceans and roaring seas that carry my name into the majestic presence of the Most High

God knows my name

I give thanks and shout outs all through the day to the Most High

In moments of grace when I am broken-hearted and feeling rejected and discouraged

In times of celebration and jubilation

In my every waking moment, in gratitude I call the names of God

Jah, Allah, Jehovah, Yawah

Like my ancestors before me and before them and down through the ages

Spirit/God knows my name

God knows my DNA

God knows every cell of my body

God knows the number of molecules in my skin and placement of every bone in my skeleton

Every wart and mole

Spirit knows my name and I know the names of the Most High

God knows my Name.

Only Begun

WILLIAM G. SINKFORD

Spirit of Life and Love, dear God of all nations:
There is so much work to do.
We have only begun to imagine justice and mercy.
Help us hold fast to our vision of what can be.
May we see the hope in our history
and find the courage and the voice
to work for that constant rebirth
of freedom and justice.
That is our dream.
Amen.

OUR SONGS

May I Be Light

MYKAL SLACK

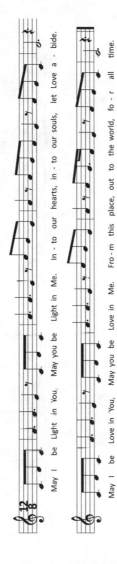

May I be Light in You. May you be Light in Me. In - to our hearts, in - to our souls, let Love a - bide.

May I be Love in You, May you be Love in Me. Fro - m this place, out to the world, fo - r all time.

This Little Light of Mine

AFRICAN AMERICAN SPIRITUAL

ARR. GLEN THOMAS RIDEOUT
VERSES 2-5 BY MYKAL SLACK

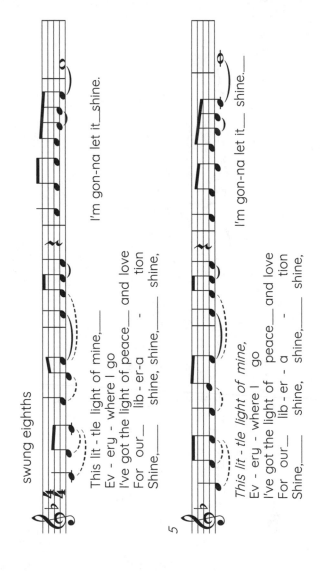

swung eighths

This lit - tle light of mine,____
Ev - ery - where I go
I've got the light of peace____ and love
For our____ lib - er - a -
Shine,____ shine, shine,____

I'm gon-na let it__shine.

This lit - tle light of mine,
Ev - ery - where I go
I've got the light of peace____ and love
For our____ lib - er - a -
Shine,____ shine, shine,____

I'm gon-na let it__ shine.____

tion
shine.

tion
shine,

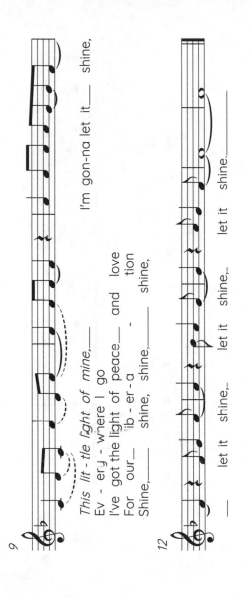

Would You Harbor Me?

YSAYE M. BARNWELL, ARR. RIDEOUT

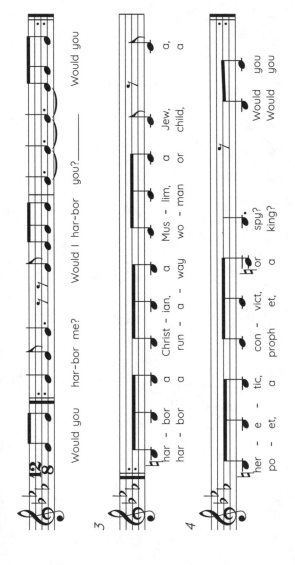

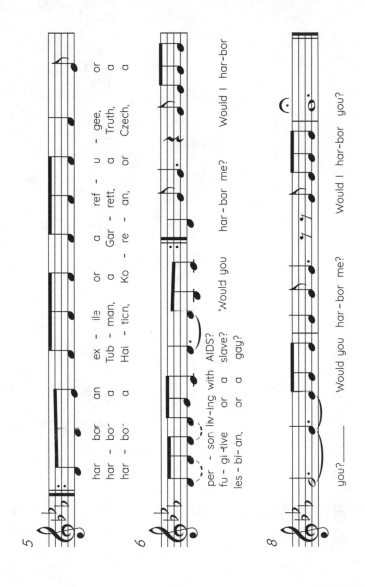

5
har - bor an ex - ile or a ref - u - gee,
har - bor a Tub - man, or a Gar - rett, a Truth,
har - bor a Hai - tian, Ko - re - an, or Czech, a

6
per - son liv - ing with AIDS? 'Would you har - bor me?
fu - gi - tive or a slave?
les - bi - an, or a gay?

8
Would you har - bor me? Would I har - bor you?
Would you har - bor me? Would I har - bor
you?_____

Hold Everybody Up!

Melanie DeMore

Verse

Just be-cause you look like you, and I look like me
Peo-ple all_ a-round the world some-times feel so sad,

does-n't mean we can't be friends, You're not my en - e - my.
but when oth - ers show_ they care, well, things don't seem so bad

da capo al segno Bridge

We go-ta Thank you Rev-'rend Doc - tor King for

show-ing_ us_ what love_ can_ bring. Thank you, thank you_ Ma

da capo al fine

- di - ba,_ for lift-ing up_ South Af - ri - ca. We got-ta

Welcome Home

Rev. Osagyefo Sekou, Jay-Marie Hill

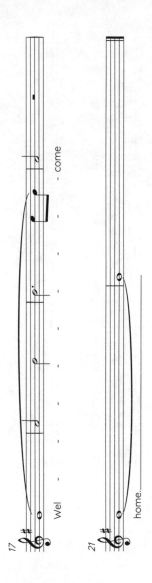

I Need You to Survive

David Frazier

OUR SACRED SPACES AND PRACICES

The Music

Everett Hoagland

This Juneteenth's soundtrack is: sirens,

march-time chanting *NO JUSTICE,*
NO PEACE, LOUD honking,

poster-plastered car caravans' blaring horns
at the intersection of yesterday, today,
tomorrow blast the wrongful

Right's Jericho walls all around us.
Loop the cities, past memorial murals
painted with blood, white lies & indivisible

video-recorded, self-evident, blued black truths
while making a way toward a perfectly pitched
modulation to a more harmonious rendition of
    America

the Beautiful, that rings truer HA! than the cracked
Liberty Bell. Because so far, since the Middle
Passage "Free Market" slave trade, as

an anthem, its truer Declaration has variously been:
a bondaged work song, yes, a "negro" spiritual,

prison labor song, strangely fruited jazz tree

I can't breathe scat, Lift Every Voice, yes, We Shall
Overcome, yes, and righteous rage-freighted rap.
The nation is again at the bridge

of an echoing crossroad blues.
An alternate lyric of something chanted
every fifty years or so. A differently similar road

song sung over and over again.
But not by just us now, with *masses*
of allies chiming in this time. Our feet meting

out march-time beats matching footfalls still
rising, reverberating from Congo Square where
long ago entranced Africans dancing freely to drum

music's congas, djembes, dun-duns moved us
righteously onward up the stony road "we trod,"
the one we have always been on. So, yes,

yet again, let us *Walk Together Children. . . .*
NO JUSTICE, YES, NO PEACE!
YES, NO JUSTICE, NO PEACE!

Peace. "A Love Supreme." So may it be. Amen.

Digital Faith

SOREN BYRD, AKA BENITA JEANELLE

I open my laptop, waiting for our service to start.

Seeking connection to the interdependent world wide web of which we all are a part.

The love from the congregation holds us tight.

Received through a series of circuits, lights, and megabytes.

Our congregation and love from across the nation beamed into my living room.

Power, hope, faith, and belonging all delivered via Zoom.

At home, I miss the steam from the coffee, the hands on my shoulder, the "excuse me, may I get by?" and the fussy babies that cry.

Yet still when the chalice is lit, the lights turn on in our souls.

There's nothing else like shared meditation for bringing us to the whole.

African Spirit

ANTHONY Y. STRINGER

The African Spirit is deeply embedded in nature, never existing apart from its material manifestations. It is the part of nature in which we perceive ultimacy, omnipresence, beneficence, omnipotence, creativity, and omniscience. Without it, nature is a meaningless landscape—there for us to despoil and rape at our pleasure. The African Spirit is equally immanent in us. Without it, we lack purpose and meaning. We cease to be ends in ourselves and readily become just another exploitable and disposable tool. Our survival, and the planet's ability to survive us, require that we never cease to perceive the spiritual essence within all things.

> There is a Spirit within nature
> and a Spirit within me.
> Perceiving Its presence,
> I am filled with joy,
> and I strive to be mindful.
> Perceiving Its grandeur,
> I am filled with reverence,

and I approach to worship.
Perceiving Its power,
I am filled with humbleness,
and I strive to be in harmony.
Perceiving Its beneficence,
I am filled with gratitude,
and I am moved to serve others.
Perceiving Its creativity,
I am filled with awe,
and I am inspired to create.
Perceiving Its mystery,
I am filled with wonder,
and the passion to discover.
This then is the Spirit within nature,
and the nature of the Spirit within me.
Ashe.

Wade in the Water

SOFÍA BETANCOURT

Wade in the Water, Children.
God's gonna trouble the
Water.

I laughed along the low
tide line at Stinson beach,
searching for absent
sand dollars among the
broken bits of shell
lining the shore.

Remembering myself and
Whose
spoils I was searching for,
I approached the Pacific,
risking a tongue-lashing from Her
wet, rolling
waters.

Touching hand from
heart to water,
returning to heart,

I made
signs of reverence—
no longer
struggling to stay dry.

I heard the rippling waves of
Her laughing voice,
mocking my frustrated searching,
amusement ripe in my failure.
Come into my waters, She
purred, *allow Me to shape you and
you may gather My gifts.*

Shape me?
Would my jagged edges
soften like the
finest beach glass—
or would I be ground into dust,
scattered among my
brethren in the duncs?

Wading in Her waters left me   transformed
in just moments.
My boots became soggy,
pants pushed above my knees,
completely saturated, no matter

how I rolled them.

And She
showered me in sand dollars—
a basketful.

I spent an hour in those waters.
Leaving Stinson Beach with the
color high in my cheeks,
pants wet to mid-thigh,
hair blown in every direction—
the unneeded pieces of myself
crumbled up, riding grittily in the
spaces between my toes.

Like a conch shell held close to the ear,
the waves' song still
sings in the open vessel of my being.

Wade in the water, Children—
wade.

Lamentations

MATHEW P. TAYLOR

Lamentations
Are the love language of the brokenhearted
Hurt and crying
For the living and dying
Lamentations are how the heart releases
The excess of emotion
Love
Anger
Disappointment
Sadness
Defeat
Desperation
Hope
Lamentations
Are the love language of Pandora's box
Holding secrets
And truths
The gentle heart
The sensitive mind
The body in motion
Living

Sometimes loving
Always working
Lamentations
Are a way to be seen
And held
And heard
For once
So that the weeping
The stories behind the tears
Are not silenced

Being UU and Black

MYA WADE-HARPER

Means watching as they put up the BLM sign
And knowing the fight has hardly started
It means being coined a token
And lifted up while you do all the work
Means late nights and meetings
Sermons that you hope they will hear
Means answering questions that you
don't want to answer
And hoping it will all be enough
It means asking for more diversity
But not appropriation
It means backlash and tight smiles
and exhaustion
But being UU and Black also means
Raising our hands and voting for justice
While friendships warm my heart
It means feeling right at home in those walls
And knowing these people understand
Means education and singing and healing
and marching in the cold together
It means knowing your dream is shared by others

and you can accomplish it together
Means chalices, rituals, and sacred spaces,
feeling welcome and loved and holy
Means supporting values that support my
people's life
It means Black spaces and spending time
healing with those who look like me
It means knowing inside that you belong even
if sometimes it is so hard and tiring
I am here to stay

Lynching Version 2.0

Ebony C. Peace

Knee on my neck a modern noose
Agitated bystanders watching, recording, shouting

Dignity cracked to pieces, faded fast into the trees
Pressed hard, viciously, my cheek into the pavement
Tears evaporated
Breath dissipated
Until breath was no more
A divine expansion

Spirit flown into the arms of my mother
Her name trembling against my thick brown lips
Politics
Heaven, stained glass, church bells, sirens
Death

Protest
Riots
Fire
Love

OUR WORK

Finding Your Way

SHERRYL N. WESTON

> *Hands that serve are holier than lips that pray.*
> —*Sai Baba*

I was a UU for ten years before I realized there was a historic black membership. Now we have DRUUMM (Diverse and Revolutionary Unitarian Universalist Multicultural Ministries) and BLUU (Black Lives of Unitarian Universalism). Those were a long time coming! I've been very active. I love what this denomination has done for me and my spiritual journey. I am hoping my story inspires other BIPOC folks to feel okay pursuing a spiritual home that is outside of our current notions of "normal."

Not every Black person is a theist or a Christian, which can be objectionable or surprising to those with limited exposure to other perspectives. Giving oneself permission to pursue an alternative can mean internal peace and quiet. It's not easy, but it's a right, not a privilege.

My main point of connection to Unitarian Universalism is its openness to many religious traditions. One of our Principles is "a free and responsible search for truth and meaning." So long as I am careful to borrow spiritual symbolism carefully, first thoroughly researching and speaking with the holders of those traditions, I can incorporate many parts of my multicultural upbringing into my spiritual life. Baha'i, Buddhism, Wicca, and Ifa: all of these and more inform my eclectic faith.

With art, music, Earth-based African and North American Indigenous and Buddhist-rooted concepts, and a clearly articulated African American humanism at my center, I am part of a long tradition of black people combining myriad cultural influences into our own relationship with the Divine.

What is your path toward your truth and meaning? Don't be afraid to find out.

Sankofa—Go Back and Get It

Jan Carpenter Tucker

Sankofa is a term from the Twi language of the Akan tribe in Ghana. It means "it is not taboo to fetch what is at risk of being left behind," or put simply, "go back and get it." Its symbol is a bird that flies with its feet forward while its head turns backward, carrying a pebble of knowledge in its beak. When we revisit Dr. King's prophetic words, we are practicing Sankofa. The lessons we learned over the past half-century need constant reiteration, examination, and determination to break through barriers to understanding and change.

My personal acts of Sankofa have to do with truth telling. I am swearing off a particular two-step dance of avoidance of the truth. Let me explain: there hangs in the air the stench of unacknowledged, uncomfortable, and ugly truths about the lived experience of people of color in these United States. When we open our hearts and mouths to tell these experiences, too often we are told by white folks that we are being unkind, indelicate, or rude to discuss such things. I have been told, "Why does everything come down to race with you?" or

"But it's not that way anymore, right?" or "I don't have a racist bone in my body!" or "I love all people, whether green, purple, or polka dotted. I just don't see color."

Hold it right there! I won't do this dance again. Before you step on my toes one more time, I'm here to tell you, "Stop it! You are hurting me." I'm telling my truth not to hurt you personally but to ask you to open your eyes to this nugget of knowledge I am in great need of sharing. I am fetching what is at risk of being left behind and asking you to examine it along with me to see what we can do differently to make our lives together less painful, more fulfilled, mutually caring, and fully appreciated.

Earlier this week I sat in on a health assessment with my mother. The interviewer asked about her parents' health, how long they lived, what they died from, and so forth. My mother started into that two-step dance around an ugly truth and I decided it was time to tell it like it is. "My grandfather died of racism," I exclaimed. He was a Black man in the South and when he fell ill, he was turned away from the white hospital. When they found a facility that would take him, it was woefully inadequate, understaffed, and unclean. While the hospital accepted Black patients, it only housed them in the basement. My grandmother found old chicken bones in the bedside drawer and had to clean them out herself. We never received a forthright answer about the actual cause of his death. Rest assured he was treated like so many other Black men in America, with disrespect and little regard for his well-being— nay, his actual *life*. My grandfather was Harvard educated with a doctorate and a well-respected professor of biology at a prestigious historically Black college. He had been a Quaker minister and headmaster of a school in Jamaica. Not that any of those facts should give him special privilege. Yet when it came to life and death for a Black man in Louisiana, his life did not matter.

Just this weekend, someone commented on my attractive diamond ring. When she asked to examine it more closely, I saw myself stepping onto that old familiar dance floor with a simple "thank you." But this ring has an ugly truth, and I shared that ugly truth with the admirer of the ring. My grandmother first showed me that ring when I was a teenager. A young Black man had brought it to her because he found it and didn't know what to do. My grandmother didn't know what to do either, because if she tried to turn it in (to whom?), one or both of them would be accused of stealing it from the white lady. You see how it was assumed to belong to a white lady even though they didn't really know who it belonged to? My grandmother put that ring in her jewelry box and there it sat for forty years. After she died, I found it and remembered the story, which she had not told anyone else all those years. I'm sorry for the white lady who lost her ring, but I am absolutely certain she participated in the same insidious system of white privilege and supremacy that would have put that young Black man in jail, or worse, for finding her ring.

Here is what I ask of you. The next time someone tells you an ugly truth, listen respectfully and believe them. Black lives matter. Decline to do the two-step dance of avoidance and ignorance. Black lives matter. Go back and get it. Get the truth, examine it, understand it. Black lives matter. Do your part to change this system of things. Do your part to remember the past so we can correct our direction as we march on into a brighter future. Someone's life depends on it.

On Blue Notes and Resolutions

Elías Ortega

Have you heard B.B. King riffing with Lucille, his guitar, sliding from bright phrases to mournful sounds, to the blues? Musically, those haunting notes are known as blue notes. The thing about blue notes is that a simple definition can't capture what they are. If I were to tell you that a blue note is either a flattened third or the seventh note on a scale, instead of the expected major interval, I have only told you part of the story and you have gotten no blues in these here words. You see, the thing about blue notes is that one has to feel more than hear them; only then can you get the blues.

This is part of the genius of our Black music: jazz, blues, gospel, hip-hop. . . . We have infused them with life beyond the notations in which they appear. We just don't play a jazz piece, we swing to it. We don't just rhyme to a beat, we deliver our lyrics with style and flair, with our unique signature through the beat. The blues is special in this regard; we have learned to feel the blues and be moved by it, and we have gained a deeper understanding of our suffering through it.

Blue notes also teach us something else: the importance of a resolution. Blue notes are flattened notes instead of the expected major note. Because of this, musically, you can't just hang on that note forever. At some point you need to let go of it and come to a resolution. It is through the resolution of the note that we can appreciate the deepness of the sorrow in the sound but also come to know, in a feeling way, that there is a way forward.

Perhaps some years are like blue notes, bending us into a mournful sound. In the span of twelve months, our lives can change in ways we can't always fathom. Years such as this one call for resolution—not the kind entered into as an end-of-year compulsion that will be given up by mid-February, but a deeper kind, the kind that in the midst of suffering and grief visited by grief, holds onto the miracles of resurrections like the dawning of a new day.

Dark Natured

MALLESSA JAMES

We come alive
>in the dark womb that is the universe.

We are called into being
>by dark forces that cannot be seen.

We are manifested
>from the dark soil of this earth.

There is wordless music
>dancing beneath the dark tones of our bodies.

There are unspeakable truths
>echoing throughout the dark recesses of our
>minds.

There are powerful revelations
>to be discovered in the dark nights of our souls.

Remember
>that whatever we hide from ourselves
>>may feed the dark monster that disguises
>>our innermost fears.

Believe
that whatever we seek within ourselves
may fuel the dark horse that chases after
our wildest dreams.

And know
that whatever we name about ourselves
may illuminate the dark secret that
confesses our true natures.

Radical Imagination

CHARLENE CARRUTHERS

Our ancestors have dreamed of this moment. Their voices sang through our rage, our joy, our pain, and our triumph:

We were made for this moment. Let our voices, our bodies, and our spirits rise up like a mighty force.

And remember that we do this. We do this for Rakia. We do this for Isla, for Mike, for Damo, for Corrine, and for future generations.

We have no choice but to fight, but to resist, and dream big. Dream big! The Black radical imagination lives and breathes and exists through us. They have called us to this moment, and we have everything that we need and more. Everything that we need and more.

It is through collective organizing that we will win. And I believe in my heart of all hearts that we will win. Because Harriet said so. Because Assata said so. Because Denmark said so. Because Ella said so. Because Fannie said so.

And because the children that I have yet to bear say so.

Resources

The Multicultural UU Worship Collection of the Sankofa Archive
uua.org/worship/collections

Racial Justice in Unitarian Universalism
uua.org/racial-justice

Worship Web's Black Lives Matter Worship Collection
uua.org/worship/collections/black-lives-matter

Cameron, Chris. "The Faith of the Future: Black Lives of Unitarian Universalism." *Race, Religion & Black Lives Matter: Essays on a Moment and a Movement*, edited by Christopher Cameron and Phillip Luke Sintiere, Vanderbilt University Press, 2021.

UUA BIPOC Groups

DRUUMM: Diverse and Revolutionary UU Multicultural Ministries
druumm.org
Facebook: The Gathering Place - DRUUMM

Finding Our Way Home Retreat for Religious
Professionals of Color
uua.org/multiculturalism/retreat

Thrive: For UU Youth and Young Adults of Color
uua.org/youth/events/multicultural
-leadership-school

BLUU: Black Lives of Unitarian Universalism

Website: Blacklivesuu.org
Twitter: @BlackLivesUU
Facebook: @BlackLivesUU
Patreon: @blacklivesuu
Medium: Black Lives UU
YouTube: @BlackLivesUU

BLUU Havens, Black UU meet-up groups, are
currently active in the following cities:

Akron, OH
Asheville, NC
Chicagoland, IL
Columbia, MD
Montclair, NJ
Philadelphia, PA
Richmond, VA
Rockville, MD